DURGA
THE FEMININE FORCE

Om KIDZ
An imprint of Om Books International

First Published in 2024 by

Om Books International

Corporate & Editorial Office
A-12, Sector 64, Noida 201 301
Uttar Pradesh, India
Phone: +91 120 477 4100
Email: editorial@ombooks.com
Website: www.ombooksinternational.com

Sales Office
107, Ansari Road, Darya Ganj
New Delhi 110 002, India
Phone: +91 11 4000 9000
Email: sales@ombooks.com

ISBN: 978-93-53769-08-6

Printed in India

10 9 8 7 6 5 4 3 2 1

Contents

Rambha and Karambha

Thousands of years ago, two asura brothers wanted to become powerful so that they could establish the asura kingdom and rule the world. So they decided to worship Yaksha, the god of natural treasures hidden in Earth. Karambha

worshipped by standing neck-deep in water,while Rambha stood in the middle of five ritual fires called *Panchagni.*

Indra, the god of war, was alarmed at the asuras' prospect to power. He took the form of a crocodile and killed Karambha. Rambha, on coming to know about his brother's death, became mad with anger and grief. He was about to give up his life, when Agni, the god of fire, appeared before him. "Do not kill yourself, son. You have no right to kill anybody, even yourself. That's a sin,"said Agni.

"Then bless me with a son whom no god or asura shall be able to kill," demanded Rambha.

"So be it. Look for a woman who wins your heart. She will bear such a child for you." Saying this, Agni disappeared. Having received his boon, Rambha did what he was told and began his search for love.

While he was roaming in the garden of Yaksha, he saw a female buffalo and fell in love with her. In order to spend time with her, he transformed himself into a male buffalo and plunged into the water. Soon, they were married.

A real male buffalo became jealous on seeing this. Blinded by his rage, he killed Rambha.

Mahishasura the Buffalo Demon

The female buffalo, who was carrying Rambha's child, decided to kill herself. But before she could end her life, she gave birth to an asura who had the head of a buffalo and the body of a man. She called him Mahishasura.

Like his father, Mahishasura also wanted to wage war upon the gods. To gain more power, Mahishasura went to the mountains and began to worship Lord Brahma, the creator of the Universe.

At last, Lord Brahma appeared before the demon and said, "I am happy with your dedication. I will grant you a wish."

"O Lord, I want to become immortal," said Mahishasura.

The Lord smiled and said, "That is not possible, son. Everybody who is born has to die. Please wish for something else."

The wicked Mahishasura promptly said, "Then bless me so that nobody can kill me except a woman."

No woman can beat me in a fight, he thought secretly.

The Lord granted him this boon and disappeared.

Mahishasura returned to his kingdom and appointed Sikshura, a ferocious asura, as the chief commander of his demon army. They began to invade all the neighbouring kingdoms and nobody could stop them.

Soon, Mahishasura called a council of his generals and told them, "Friends, now that we have conquered earth, let's shift focus on our arch-enemies, the gods.

Let's invade Amravathi, the capital of Indra, tomorrow morning."

Mahishasura's messenger met Indra and told him about Mahishasura's intention of war. Indra, worried, called a quick meeting with the principal gods, i.e., Yama, the god of death, Vayu the god of wind, Varuna the god of water and sky, and Agni the god of fire.

The gods immediately sprang up from their seats. “How dare he!” said one. “We must not surrender. We will fight. We will teach them a lesson!” said another. And the battle began.

Thousands of demons began to fight against the gods. Nothing could be heard except war cries from both sides, swords clashing, horses neighing and elephants trumpeting.

The gods began to win in the beginning. They killed many asuras and scared many more away.

When Mahishasura saw that one of his favourite warriors had fallen on the battlefield and died, he created thousands of clones of his own self. These clones then rushed at the gods who could not make out who the real Mahishasura was. They began to run helter-skelter. Until then, Brahma, Vishnu and Shiva were watching only from a distance. Now Indra asked them for help.

Immediately, the three most powerful gods appeared on the battlefield. Vishnu came forward and banged Mahishasura on the head with his famous mace, *Kaumodaki.* Stunned by the mighty blow, Mahishasura fell down.

He transformed himself into a lion and charged at Vishnu. Protected by Brahma's boon, Mahishasura hit Vishnu and knocked him down. The Lord retired from the battlefield and took refuge in Vaikunttha, his abode.

Lord Shiva and Lord Brahma also realised that their efforts would bear no fruit. So they, too, left the battlefield.

Watching their heroes flee the battlefield, the gods lost all hope. Indra tried to encourage them, but to no avail.

Mahishasura then assumed the form of a giant buffalo and attacked the gods with his horns and hooves.

All the brave gods ran away, including Indra himself.

The jubilant army of Mahishasura entered Amravathi without anybody trying to stop them. Mahishasura sat on the great throne of the king of heaven.

He appointed his trusted generals in the posts previously held by the principal gods. The poor gods were thrown out of Heaven.

They met Lord Brahma and pleaded, "Save us from this lowly life! O Brahma, please save us!" Lord Brahma said, "Only a woman can help us here. Let's go and seek Lord Shiva's opinion."

Lord Shiva listened to their worries and said, "I can't think of a way out. With Brahma's blessings protecting him, Mahishasura is invincible. We must seek Lord Vishnu's help."

When they approached Vishnu, he smiled and said, “We tried to kill him in battle. Not only did he survive, but also, all of us had to flee the battlefield.

Only a woman can kill him, but until now, there is no woman who can cause his death. Let us create a woman using the best of all our powers. This lady will be able to kill Mahishasura."

As Vishnu proposed this idea, a dazzling streak of light emerged from the face of Brahma and filled the dark sky with its brilliance. It was as bright as the Sun and as red as sapphire. Lord Shiva created a silver coloured flame that joined the light of Brahma. Finally, Vishnu contributed his power to this force in the form of light.

A beautiful woman emerged out of that light. They called her Devi Durga.

Vishnu said, "Let us give all our special weapons to her. We should arm her adequately for the battle against Mahishasura."

Saying this, he gave her his discus. Shiva gave her his trident. All other gods contributed in some form or the other.

All the gods present there said, "O Mother Goddess, you are Heaven, you are Earth, you are the Eternal Principle, you are the great Eternal Truth. You are our only hope!"

The Devi mounted on a lion and marched towards Amravathi.

As she reached Amravathi, she roared out a loud cry that shook the ground. Mahishasura, startled, turned to one of his advisors and said, “Who dares to shout and disturb my peace? Go and find out at once.”

When the advisors came outside, they were stunned by what they saw. A graceful woman was coming towards them, riding a fierce-looking lion. They informed their King about what they had seen outside.

"Oh that's interesting!" said the wicked king of the asuras, "Go and bring her here. I will marry her and she will be my queen."

Durga Takes Revenge

Mahishasura's prime minister took a small band of soldiers and went to the goddess. He said to her, "Who are you? My King, the great Mahishasura, wants to meet you."

"Sure!" said Devi Durga, "I want to meet him too. But I am not here to be his guest. I have come to kill him and get the three worlds rid of such a monster!"

The prime minister was greatly surprised. “I have never heard such words from any woman. You must be out of your mind. I would advise you to please not cause trouble, and come with us. It is a great honour that Mahishasura has been impressed by your beauty. Marry him and be our queen.”

“Go back and tell him Devi Durga challenges him to a battle. Either he comes out to face me, or he goes back where he has come from.”

The bemused minister did not know what to say. He went back to Mahishasura and told him what had transpired between him and the unknown woman.

Mahishashura then turned to his favourite general, Tamra, and said, "Go to this woman and humble her pride. Do not harm her because she will be your queen. Use your subtle skills and the art of illusion. Capture her and bring her to the court."

Tamra set out to carry his master's orders. He took an army of demons with him.

As soon as Durga saw Tamra, she gave out a loud cry, drawing from all the wells of energy within her.

Tamra trembled to hear that deafening noise and came back. “O Lord, she is no ordinary woman. I do not know what to do.”

Asura Bakshala rose from his seat and said, "O Tamra, stop this nonsense. Let me go and face this woman. I will drag her to the court."

However, Durga easily killed him with her trident.

Durmukha took charge after this. Durga shot at his chariot and it turned over, throwing Durmukha on the ground.

Durmukha lurched forward and hit the lion with his mace. Immediately, Durga took out her sword and chopped his head off.

Hearing about Durmukha's death, Mahishasura sprang up from his throne. "Do you mean to say that a woman has killed the mighty Durmukha and Bakshala?"

Next, he sent Sikshura along with Tamra. Tamra tried to hit her lion with an iron rod. Furious, the goddess cut his head with her sword.

Then Durga shot five arrows at Sikshura. The first arrow hit his sword and broke it into pieces. The second arrow cut off his hand. The other three arrows cut his head off that fell on the ground.

Asiloma and Bidala, two of Mahishasura's most trusted warriors, then jumped into the fray. Durga's lion tore off Asiloma's chest with his claws. And Durga beheaded Bidala with her sword.

This created much panic among the asuras. They began to run here and there as had happened with the gods' army earlier. Durga merely smiled at them and waited for Mahishasura, their chief, to come out of his palace.

Finally, Mahishasura himself came out in a huff. Though he was angry, he repeated his marriage proposal one last time.

But Devi Durga was in no mood for such things. She said, "I have no wish to become your queen, demon! Either you retire to your place in hell, or prepare to die."

Mahishasura could take no more from her. He lunged forth with his devious weapons and the final showdown began. He shot a volley of arrows at Durga, but she easily countered them with her arrows.

Mahishasura, then, took the form of a lion and charged at Durga's lion-mount.

The angry Goddess struck him with her lethal arrows that looked like serpents. Yelling in rage and pain, Mahishasura changed himself to a huge elephant.

The elephant-form Mahishasura uprooted huge blocks of rock with his trunk and hurled them at Durga.

Durga's lethal arrows broke them into pieces in mid-air. Suddenly, Durga's lion jumped at Mahishasura and clawed at his forehead, tearing it apart Mahishasura began to bleed profusely.

Finally, Mahishasura came back to his original form, that of half–buffalo and half–asura.

They fought a fierce battle, using all their weapons against each other. Durga struck him valiantly with her trident. She pierced his body straight through the heart. Then she chopped his head off with her discus. Thus Durga killed the evil monster and restored peace and prosperity.

The Story of Gauri

After Goddess Durga slew Mahishasura, she took birth as a human being. Her father was called Daksha and she came to be known as Gauri. She was also called Sati. Right from childhood, she showed great devotion to Lord Shiva. When she grew up, she wanted to marry him.

Daksha did not approve of this. He said, “I will never let you marry someone like Shiva, who is nothing but a dirty, roaming ascetic. He lives with spirits and ghosts.”

Daksha's disapproval could not stop Gauri from wooing Lord Shiva. She left the life of luxury at the palace of Daksha and went to the forest. There she began to worship Shiva.

She undertook a most austere life. Slowly, she gave up her meals and deprived herself of all earthly pleasures, so engrossed was she in her prayers. This impressed Lord Shiva and finally he appeared before Sati and said, "I am very pleased with your dedication and I accept you as my bride."

Since Daksha was totally against the marriage, he wanted to insult Shiva on the slightest pretext. He arranged a grand sacrifice and there he invited all the gods except Shiva. Gauri, now Shiva's wife, was very keen to visit her friends and relatives on this occasion and insisted on visiting her father. Shiva could easily see that the intention of Daksha was to insult him, and in his absence if Gauri visited her father, he would insult her too. He asked her not to go, but she wouldn't listen.

As expected, Daksha heaped all sorts of insults on Gauri, and all his harsh words were related to Lord Shiva. Unable to bear her husband's insult, she set herself on fire and ended her life.

The moment this news reached Shiva, he stormed into Daksha's sacrificial ceremony and killed him immediately. Then he took up Gauri's charred body on his shoulders and began the most destructive dance the world had ever seen. This dance came to be known as *Tandava.*

All the gods rushed to Vishnu, "O Vishnu, please stop Shiva's Tandava! Or he will destroy all creation around us."

Vishnu shot his discus at Gauri's body and cut it into 51 pieces. All the pieces fell in different parts of the world. As the charred body of Gauri was now removed from Lord Shiva's sight, he came back to his senses. He calmed down and gave life back to all that he had killed in a rage.

Gauri, or Sati, later took another birth. This time she came to be known as Parvati. She united with Shiva in her second birth and they are believed to have a happy family on Mount Kailash.

OTHER TITLES IN THIS SERIES

9 789384 225049

9 789392 834387

9 789392 834516

9 789392 834523

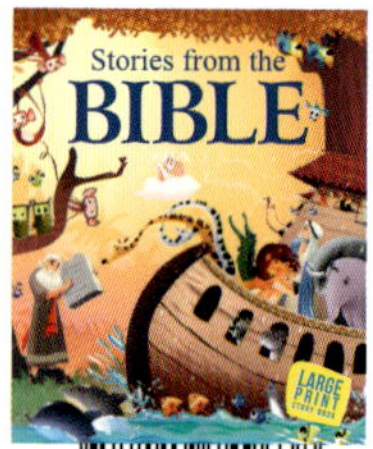

9 788119 749638

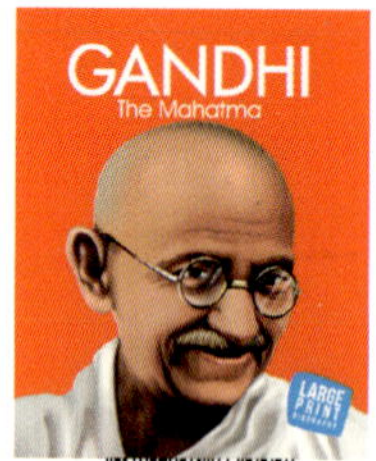

9 789392 834448

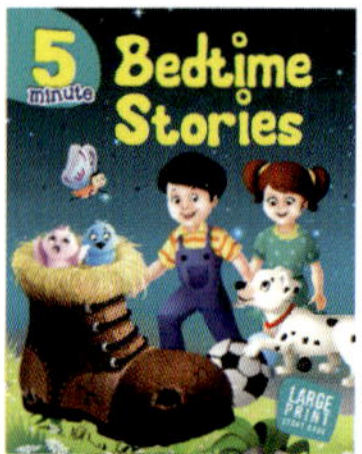

9 789392 834530

9 789392 834431

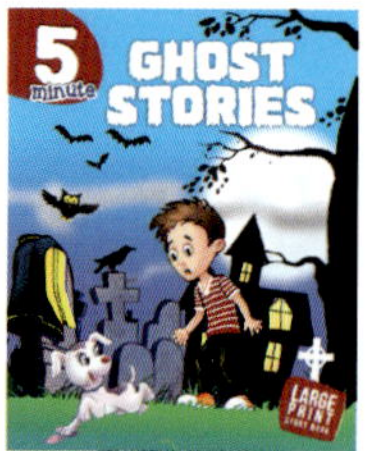

9 789394 547902

9 789394 54788

9 789394 547896

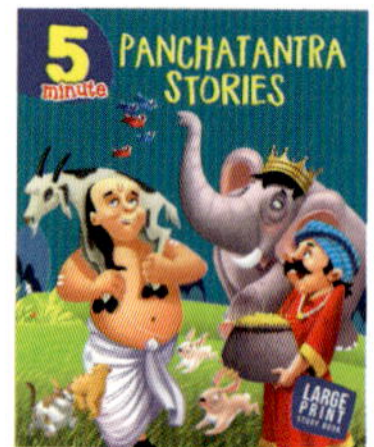

9 789394 547926

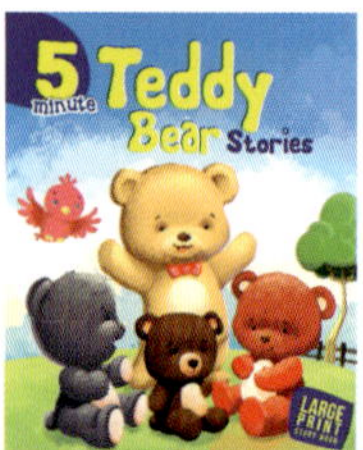

9 789386 108333

9 788196 010904

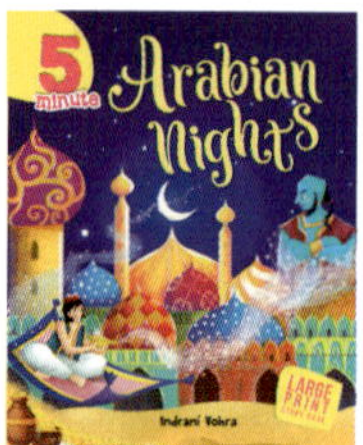

9 789385 273025

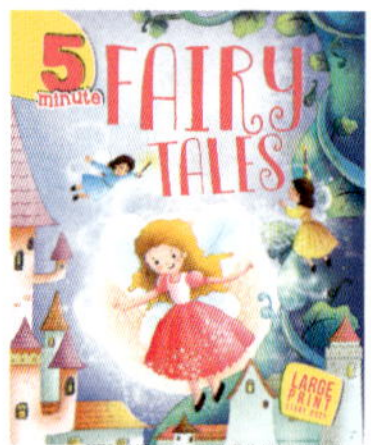

9 789382 607885

9 788119 749720

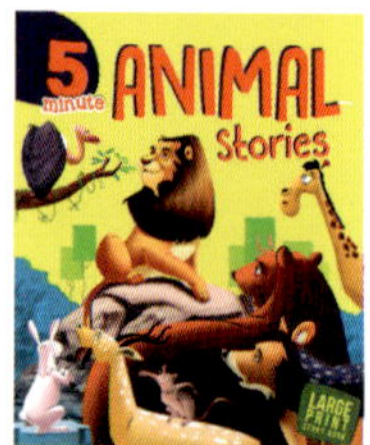

9 789382 607878

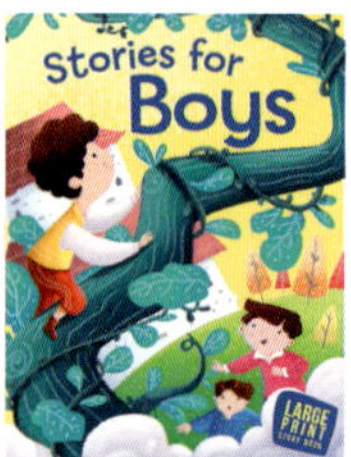

9 789381 607428

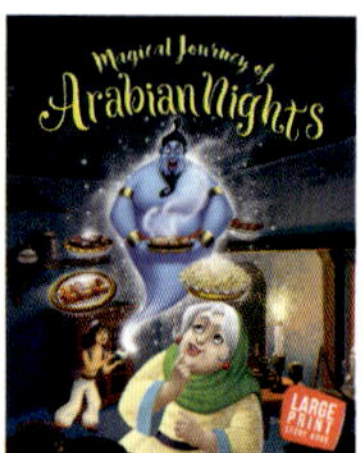

9 789394 54795

9 789394 547971

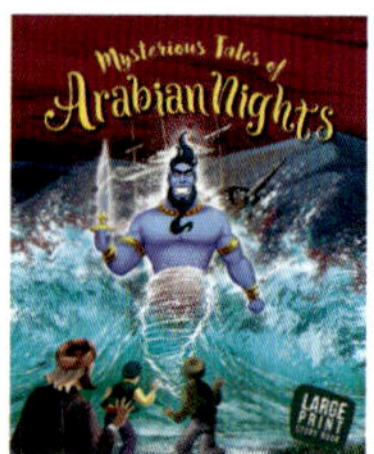

9 789394 547988

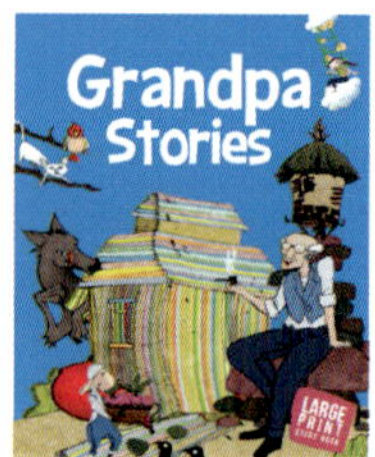

9 789392 834073

9 789394 547940

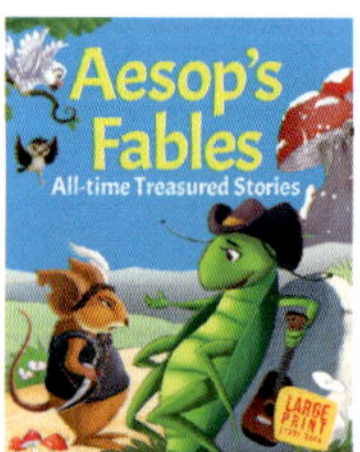

9 789392 834455

9 789392 834462

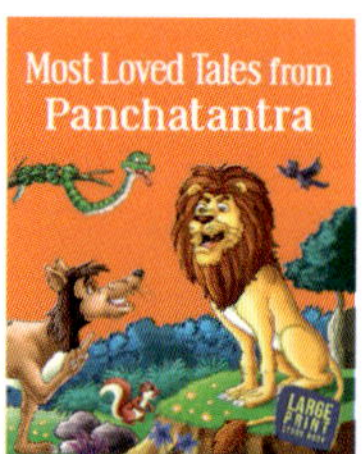

9 789392 834158

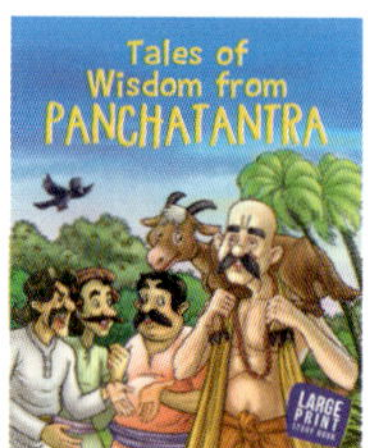

9 789394 547995

9 789394 547964

9 789394 04601